# Alberta

# Alberta

Sarah Yates

Lerner Publications Company

LIBRARY OF CONGRESS
CATALOGING-IN-PUBLICATION DATA

Yates, Sarah.
    Alberta / by Sarah Yates.
        p. cm. — (Hello Canada)
    Includes index.
    ISBN 0-8225-2763-4 (lib. bdg.)
    1. Alberta—Juvenile literature. [1. Alberta.]
I. Title. II. Series.
F1076.4.Y38  1995
971.23—dc20                              94-45478
                                              CIP
                                               AC

Manufactured in the United States of America

1 2 3 4 5 6 – JR – 00 99 98 97 96 95

Cover photograph by Steve Warble/Mountain Magic. Background photo by R. Chen/SuperStock.

The glossary on page 68 gives definitions of words shown in **bold type** in the text.

**Senior Editor**
Gretchen Bratvold
**Editor**
Domenica Di Piazza
**Photo Researcher**
Cindy Hartmon
**Series Designer**
Steve Foley
**Designer**
Darren Erickson

*Our thanks to Patricia Myers, David Leonard, and Michael Payne from the Historic Sites and Archives Service of Alberta Community Development for their help in preparing this book.*

 This book is printed on acid-free, recyclable paper.

# Contents

*The Easter egg in Vegreville is called a pysanka in Ukrainian. Many Ukrainians came to Alberta in the early 1900s.*

# Fun Facts

Vegreville, Alberta, is home to the world's largest Easter egg. The colorful aluminum egg, which weighs 5,000 pounds (2,270 kilograms), measures 26 feet (8 meters) in length and 18 feet (5m) in width. It was built in 1975 to mark the 100th anniversary of the formation of the Royal Canadian Mounted Police in Alberta.

The area surrounding the city of Lethbridge in southern Alberta is known for its strong winds. Albertans joke that if you lean to one side, you must be from Lethbridge.

🍁 With an average of 2,000 hours of sun per year, Alberta is the sunniest province in Canada.

Hi! My name is Barkley. As you read *Alberta*, I will be helping you make sense of some of the maps and charts that appear in the book.

🍁 On the back of the Canadian $10 bill is a picture of Moraine Lake in Alberta's Banff National Park. Surrounded by 10 mountain peaks, the lake is one of the most photographed bodies of water in the province.

🍁 Wood Buffalo National Park in northern Alberta is home to the world's largest herd of free-roaming wood buffalo.

🍁 Alberta—known as the Princess Province—was named after Princess Louise Caroline Alberta. The princess was the daughter of Queen Victoria, who ruled Great Britain from 1837 to 1901.

# *A Royal Province*

Alberta is a land of majestic mountain peaks, sprawling cattle ranches, bustling cities, and gently rolling farmland. Vast stretches of **prairie,** or grasslands, cover much of the province, which is the westernmost of Canada's three Prairie Provinces. Farms and ranches on the prairies in Alberta produce much of Canada's grain and cattle. In addition, rich deposits of oil, natural gas, and coal make Alberta the top mining region in the nation.

Nearly twice as big as Japan, Alberta is the sixth largest of Canada's provinces and territories. British Columbia lies to the west and to the east is Saskatchewan. The vast Northwest Territories sprawls along Alberta's northern boundary, and the U.S. state of Montana forms Alberta's southern border.

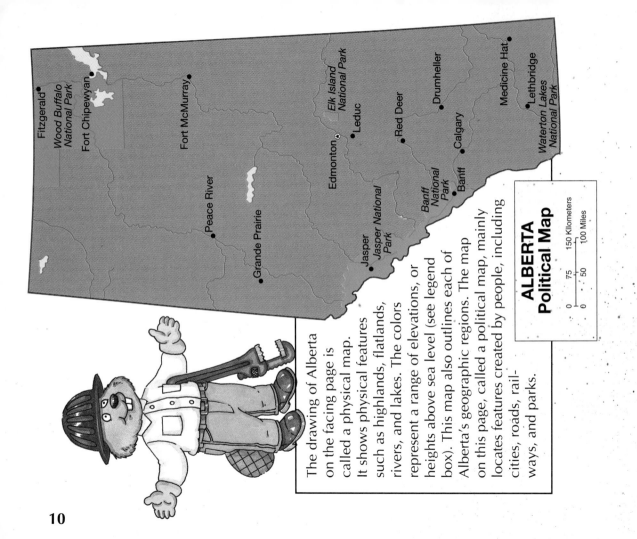

The drawing of Alberta on the facing page is called a physical map. It shows physical features such as highlands, flatlands, rivers, and lakes. The colors represent a range of elevations, or heights above sea level (see legend box). This map also outlines each of Alberta's geographic regions. The map on this page, called a political map, mainly locates features created by people, including cities, roads, railways, and parks.

**ALBERTA**
**Political Map**

| 0 | 75 | 150 Kilometers |
|---|---|---|
| 0 | 50 | 100 Miles |

Fitzgerald

Wood Buffalo
National Park

Fort Chipewyan

Fort McMurray

Peace River

Grande Prairie

Jasper

Jasper National
Park

Edmonton

Leduc

Elk Island
National Park

Red Deer

Drumheller

Medicine Hat

Lethbridge

Banff
National
Park

Banff

Calgary

Waterton Lakes
National Park

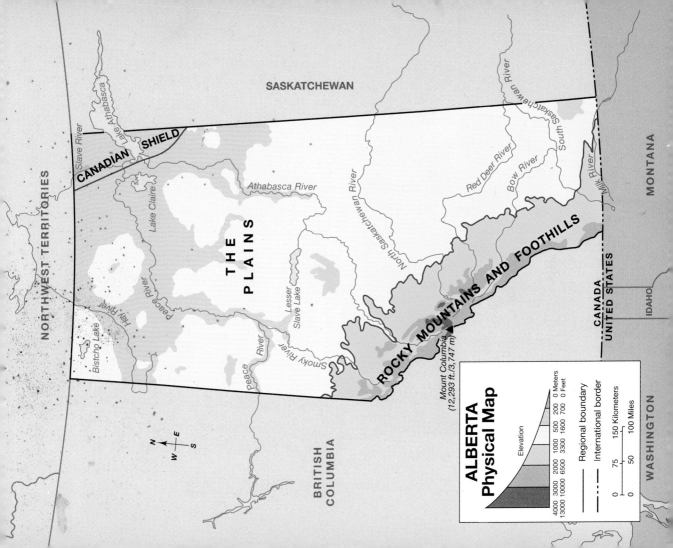

SASKATCHEWAN

NORTHWEST TERRITORIES

CANADIAN SHIELD

Lake Athabasca

Slave River

Athabasca River

Lake Claire

Peace River

Hay River

Bistcho Lake

THE PLAINS

Lesser Slave Lake

Smoky River

Peace River

North Saskatchewan River

Red Deer River

Bow River

South Saskatchewan River

Milk River

ROCKY MOUNTAINS AND FOOTHILLS

Mount Columbia
(12,293 ft./3,747 m)

MONTANA

IDAHO

CANADA
UNITED STATES

WASHINGTON

BRITISH COLUMBIA

N
E
S
W

**ALBERTA**
**Physical Map**

Elevation

| 4000 | 13000 |
| 3000 | 10000 |
| 2000 | 6500 |
| 1000 | 3300 |
| 500 | 1600 |
| 200 | 700 |
| 0 Meters | 0 Feet |

—— Regional boundary
—··— International border

0      75      150 Kilometers
0      50      100 Miles

*Shaped by wind and rain, columns of rock called hoodoos rise along the Bow River in southwestern Alberta.*

During the last **Ice Age,** which ended about 10,000 years ago, a huge mass of ice called an **ice cap** covered much of Alberta. The ice cap scoured the landscape and gouged deep holes in the land. Rain and the water from melting ice eventually filled the holes, creating lakes. The ice cap also ground up rocks and deposited soil across much of the region.

High in the cold mountains along Alberta's western border is the Columbia Icefield, a huge sheet of ice left over from the Ice Age. The Columbia Icefield is the source of about 30 **glaciers** (masses of ice that move through mountain valleys), and its melting waters feed several major river systems. For this reason, the icefield is sometimes called the Mother of Rivers.

Flowing from the Columbia Icefield,

*Melting ice from a glacier forms the North Saskatchewan River.*

the Athabasca River heads east and north to Lake Athabasca, Alberta's largest lake. Other big lakes include Bistcho, Claire, and Lesser Slave. Lake Louise in Banff National Park is world famous for its blue-green water.

Major rivers in northern Alberta include the Peace, the Smoky, the Slave, and the Hay. The North Saskatchewan River, which also begins in the Columbia Icefield, runs across central Alberta. The Bow, the South Saskatchewan, and the Milk Rivers cross the southern part of the province.

*Bighorn sheep* (above) ***and mountain goats*** (inset, top) ***climb in the Rocky Mountains,
where Indian paintbrush*** (inset, bottom) ***and other wildflowers bloom.***

Alberta has three land regions—the Rocky Mountains, the Plains, and the Canadian Shield. Formed millions of years ago, the Rocky Mountains (or Rockies) rise like a rock wall along the southwestern edge of the province. The peaks are part of the vast Rocky Mountain system, which stretches from the U.S. state of Alaska, through western Canada, and down across much of the western United States.

Many of the region's peaks are snowcapped all year long. High up the mountainsides, where the weather is too cold for trees to grow, surefooted mountain goats and bighorn sheep graze on shrubs, mosses, and other low-growing plants. Farther down the slopes, grizzly bears, eagles, and moose make their homes in forests of fir, spruce, and birch trees. In wide mountain valleys, wildflowers such as saxifrage and fireweed grow. Crystal-clear lakes mirror the peaks above.

Streams flow across the foothills at the base of the Rockies. Logging is important in the northern foothills, where aspen, balsam fir, poplar, and spruce trees are plentiful. Cattle graze in the southern foothills.

*The treeless land atop high mountains is called tundra. Only hardy, small plants can survive the cold, windy climate there.*

*Alberta's provincial flower—the wild rose* (inset, far right)—*grows throughout the Plains* (right), *where coyotes* (above) *and other animals make their homes.*

The flat prairies that span central Alberta make up most of the Plains, the province's largest region. Although the northern part of the Plains is hilly and forested, few trees grow in the rest of the region. Pronghorn antelope, mule deer, coyotes, and foxes roam the Plains.

Most of Canada's oil and natural gas come from the Plains region. Much of the southern part of the Plains is plowed under to plant vast fields of wheat and other crops. Ranchers raise cattle and sheep as well. Alberta's two major cities—Calgary and Edmonton (the province's capital)—are located in the Plains. Smaller cities in the region include Lethbridge, Medicine Hat, and Red Deer.

*The Canadian Shield is rich in minerals such as gold, nickel, zinc, and copper.*

The northeastern corner of Alberta is covered by a small section of the Canadian Shield, a vast region of ancient rock that stretches across much of northern Canada. Few people live in this remote part of Alberta, where winters are very cold. Communities in the region include Fort Chipewyan and Fitzgerald.

The weather in Alberta varies greatly from north to south. Summers are warm and dry on the southern plains, where average July temperatures are usually above 64° F (18° C). In some parts of northern Alberta, on the other hand, summer temperatures can fall below 50° F (10° C). Winters are long and cold throughout the province but are harsher in the north. Average winter temperatures there can plunge below –8° F (–22° C). Winter readings in southern Alberta are much warmer, averaging above 10° F (–12° C).

As much as 24 inches (61 centimeters) of **precipitation** (rain and snow) may fall in the foothills of the Rockies each year, but the rest of the province is drier. About 18 inches (46 cm) of rain and snow fall in the north. Southeastern Alberta receives only 12 inches (30 cm) of precipitation annually.

Periodically throughout the year, warm winds called **chinooks** blow into Alberta from the Pacific Ocean, which lies to the west. Chinooks can raise temperatures quickly—sometimes by as much as 40° F (22° C) in just 15 minutes! In the winter, a chinook wind can melt snow within hours. When this happens, many Albertans peel off their ski pants and put on shorts to enjoy the sudden change in weather.

*Even in summer, snow covers Alberta's mountain peaks.*

# *From Indians to Immigrants*

The first people to live in what is now Alberta left behind neither buildings nor books. They recorded their lives by drawing pictures on cliffs and other stone surfaces and by passing on spoken legends from generation to generation. Some of the stories tell of the creation of these people on the North American continent.

Many scientists think these Aboriginal, or Native, peoples came to North America from Asia at least 10,000 years ago. The Aboriginals probably crossed a land bridge that once connected the two continents.

Traveling on foot, their descendants spent most of their time looking for food. At sites called buffalo jumps, hunters drove herds of buffalo over cliffs. At the bottom, families butchered the dead animals and processed the meat for use throughout the year. Hides, bones, and buffalo hair were used to make clothing, tools, and weapons.

*More than 1,000 years ago, Aboriginal artists drew pictures on rock surfaces at what is now Writing-on-Stone Provincial Park.*

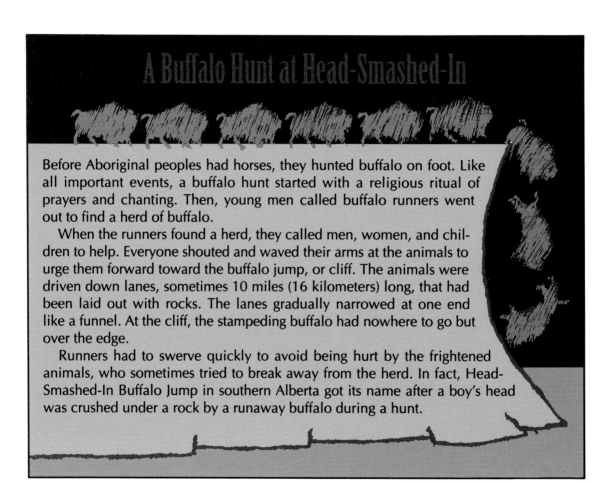

# A Buffalo Hunt at Head-Smashed-In

Before Aboriginal peoples had horses, they hunted buffalo on foot. Like all important events, a buffalo hunt started with a religious ritual of prayers and chanting. Then, young men called buffalo runners went out to find a herd of buffalo.

When the runners found a herd, they called men, women, and children to help. Everyone shouted and waved their arms at the animals to urge them forward toward the buffalo jump, or cliff. The animals were driven down lanes, sometimes 10 miles (16 kilometers) long, that had been laid out with rocks. The lanes gradually narrowed at one end like a funnel. At the cliff, the stampeding buffalo had nowhere to go but over the edge.

Runners had to swerve quickly to avoid being hurt by the frightened animals, who sometimes tried to break away from the herd. In fact, Head-Smashed-In Buffalo Jump in southern Alberta got its name after a boy's head was crushed under a rock by a runaway buffalo during a hunt.

By the 1600s, many different Aboriginal peoples were living in what is now Alberta. The Blackfoot—which consisted of the Blackfoot, the Blood, and the Peigan nations—made their homes on the plains of southern Alberta. The three groups shared the same language and many customs. The Sarcee, the Gros Ventre, the Cree, and the Assiniboine also lived on the plains. Together these and other nations are known as the Plains Indians.

Like their ancestors, the Plains Indians depended on buffalo for food and materials. During the hunting season, families followed buffalo herds across the plains. Men hunted the animals, while women scraped and tanned the hides to make clothing and coverings for cone-shaped dwellings called tepees. Women also dried the meat and pounded it with berries and animal fat to make a long-lasting food called pemmican.

*Tepees were lightweight and easy for Blackfoot hunters to put up and take down during buffalo hunts on the plains.*

23

In the forests north of the plains lived the Slavey, the Beaver, the Chipewyan, and the Woods Cree nations. These Woodland groups depended mainly on caribou for food, clothing, and shelter. Woodland peoples also fished, hunted deer and moose, and gathered berries, roots, and bark for making food and medicine.

The Rocky Mountains were home to the Kootenay nation. These people fished the mountain streams. In the fall, the Kootenay hunted buffalo on the plains.

In the 1700s, European fur traders began seeking fur-bearing animals such as beavers, bears, mink, foxes, and otters in what is now western Canada. Many of the traders worked for a large British firm called the Hudson's Bay Company. The king of England had granted

*A Chipewyan woman* (above) *discusses a peace agreement with a group of Woods Cree people. The two nations were longtime enemies. Anthony Henday* (facing page, center) *was the first European known to have visited what is now Alberta.*

the company a vast area of land that bordered Hudson Bay, a large inland sea in eastern Canada. This territory, known as Rupert's Land, included what is now central and southern Alberta.

In 1754 the Hudson's Bay Company sent Anthony Henday to the region to try to persuade the Blackfoot to trap fur-bearing animals in exchange for manufactured goods such as copper pots, rifles, axes, and blankets. Beaver pelts were especially valuable to the company because they were used to make expensive hats in Europe.

Soon after Henday's journey, Peter Pond traveled to the area. He worked for the North West Company, a fur-trading outfit that competed with the Hudson's Bay Company.

Pond built a fur-trading post on the Athabasca River in 1778. This post, the first in what is now Alberta, was so successful that the North West Company constructed many more, including Fort Chipewyan on Lake Athabasca.

Soon the two rival companies had built forts throughout what are now central and northern Alberta. In 1821 the firms decided to merge, keeping the Hudson's Bay Company's name.

Fall and spring were exciting times at the trading posts. Each September the Hudson's Bay Company sent supplies to the posts. After a ceremony of pipe smoking, speeches,

and exchanging gifts, supplies were passed out to Aboriginal traders. In return the Indian traders promised to bring furs to the posts the following spring. When spring came, British traders collected the pelts and sent them back to the company's fort at Hudson Bay.

Many European traders married Indian women, who taught their language and customs to their husbands. Their children, called Métis, eventually became an important part of the fur trade. The Métis supplied the posts with buffalo hides and made pemmican from buffalo meat for trappers to eat while in the wilderness.

*Fur traders* (right) *transported goods by canoe to fur-trading posts such as Fort Chipewyan* (facing page) *in what is now northern Alberta. Guns, knives, metal pots, liquor, clothing, and other European items were then exchanged for furs.*

27

Contact with Europeans also harmed Aboriginals. For example, smallpox and other diseases carried to North America by Europeans killed thousands of Aboriginals. Swept by illness, some Indian nations lost more than three-fourths of their people.

More changes came in the 1840s, when **missionaries** from Europe and eastern Canada arrived to teach the Christian religion. The missionaries persuaded Aboriginals to send their sons and daughters to mission schools, which separated the children from their families. Many missionaries also tried to convince Aboriginals to give up their traditional hunting and trapping lifestyle for full-time farming. In the process, many Aboriginals lost touch with their traditional cultures.

*A group of Aboriginal children pose in European dress. They have just participated in their first communion, an important part of the Christian church service.*

*U.S. traders built Fort Whoop-Up in southern Alberta in 1869 to trade whiskey to Aboriginal peoples for furs.*

In 1867 four British **colonies,** or settlements, in what is now southeastern Canada formed a new nation called the Dominion of Canada. To expand the Dominion, Canada bought Rupert's Land from the Hudson's Bay Company in 1870. That same year, Canada also gained control of the vast North-western Territory, which lay to the north and west of Rupert's Land.

The two western regions were known together as the North-West Territories.

Meanwhile U.S. fur traders were heading for Blackfoot territory in what is now Alberta to exchange whiskey for furs and buffalo robes. The alcohol triggered violence and caused serious health problems for many Indian peoples, who had rarely been exposed to the liquor.

In 1873 a group of U.S. and Canadian wolf hunters grew angry when some of their horses were stolen. Seeking revenge, the hunters attacked a peaceful camp of Assiniboine Indians in the Cypress Hills of southeastern Alberta. The wolfers had no proof that the Assiniboine had stolen their horses, but the wolfers killed and wounded many men, women, and children. After this massacre, the Canadian government sent the newly formed North-West Mounted Police to help stop the violence in the area.

In 1874 the Canadian government sent the North-West Mounted Police (or Mounties) to establish law and order in the region. The Mounties quickly built police posts at Fort Macleod and near what are now the cities of Calgary and Edmonton and put an end to the illegal whiskey trade.

By this time, the Canadian government was encouraging people to settle in western Canada. To link the west to eastern Canada, the government planned to build a railroad across the country. The railroad project would provide jobs. Trains would bring settlers west and could also transport timber and minerals from the North-West Territories to factories in eastern Canada.

To gain land for building the railway, the Canadian government worked to persuade Aboriginal peoples to give up their territories. In exchange, government **treaties** (agreements) promised money, food, education, farm equipment, and small **reserves,** or land to be set aside for Aboriginals.

Many Aboriginals did not want to leave their land. But some saw that they had no other choice. Because fur traders and hunters had killed so many buffalo and other types of game, few of the animals remained. Without the game, Aboriginal groups could not survive following their traditional lifestyle. Most tribes in the region eventually signed the treaties and moved to reserves.

By 1883 workers for the Canadian Pacific Railway had laid tracks as far west as Calgary. Ranchers soon came to raise beef cattle on the area's grasslands. As ranching grew, so did Calgary.

Meat-packing plants were built in the town to butcher and process cattle. The beef was sent by train to markets in eastern Canada or was sold locally to feed Indians on reserves, Mounties, and railroad workers. Ranchers came to town to deposit their earnings in Calgary's banks, to buy goods in the town's stores, and to meet with fellow ranchers.

After railroads (facing page) *were built across the Rockies in the 1880s, tourists began coming to Alberta to see the mountains in Banff—Canada's first national park. To identify their cattle, which wandered freely across the plains* (below), *ranchers branded the animals* (right) *with their ranch's symbol.*

34

*Railroad companies printed colorful posters* (right) *to attract people to what is now Alberta. Farms in the region offered the newcomers jobs harvesting wheat* (facing page), *the major crop of the plains.*

Other settlers headed to the region to farm the land. Wheat was the major crop, but farmers also grew barley, oats, and potatoes. Some of the farmers were Mormons, or members of the Church of Jesus Christ of Latter-day Saints. The Mormons had left the United States seeking religious freedom in southern Alberta. **Immigrants** from Great Britain, Iceland, Sweden, Norway, Germany, and Ukraine settled in the region, too. So did people from the eastern provinces of Canada.

# A Profitable Province

In the early 1900s, settlers in the North-West Territories wanted the region to become a province. Residents of a province had more control over their affairs. Also, provinces received more money from the Canadian government than territories did. In 1905, after much discussion, the Canadian government carved two new provinces—Alberta and Saskatchewan—from part of the North-West Territories. The city of Edmonton became Alberta's capital.

Most people in the new province of Alberta farmed for a living. They sent their crops to market on trains, which were fueled by coal. Settlers also depended on coal to heat their homes. Because Alberta had rich deposits of this mineral, coal mining grew rapidly in the province during the early 1900s.

*Many Ukrainians from Eastern Europe settled in Alberta, where they built homes and churches* (facing page).

Jobs in Alberta's coal mines attracted many new immigrants from Great Britain, Czechoslovakia, Italy, and other European countries. But mining was a low-paying, dangerous job. Poisonous gases built up in the underground mines, sometimes leading to fatal explosions. Breathing thick clouds of coal dust often gave miners a deadly disease known as black lung.

Hoping to improve working conditions, coal miners in Alberta joined unions (workers' organizations). The unions organized strikes, during which union members refused to work unless the company owners provided safer working conditions and better wages. By 1906 miners had gained an increase in pay, and a new law was passed to help workers and employers settle future disagreements.

# Life in a Hutterite colony

Hutterites, a German-speaking group, first arrived in Alberta in 1918. They followed the Christian teachings of Jakob Hutter, who had founded the religious group in Central Europe in 1528.

Hutterites believe in simple living and are against war and all violence. They live and farm on land they own together. In Hutterite villages, called colonies, families have their own apartments. Everyone in the colony works together, and the children go to colony schools. Hutterites grow vegetables and fruit and raise livestock. They shop and sell their farm goods in cities and towns.

In Alberta, the Canadian government promised the Hutterites freedom to live according to their religion. But during World War II (1939-1945), some Albertans were angry that the Hutterites could stay home to farm and earn money while other Albertans were fighting overseas. Fearing violence against the Hutterites, Alberta decided where the colonies could be located and limited the amount of land Hutterites could own. This law was in force until 1972. Nowadays Alberta has more than 100 Hutterite colonies.

A **drought,** or long period of dry weather, hit Alberta in the late 1920s and lasted throughout most of the 1930s. With little or no rain, Alberta's prairies became so parched that crops withered and died. Dust storms blew away valuable topsoil. Without earnings from crops, many farmers were forced to leave their farms.

*So many dust storms hit Alberta during the depression that the era was called the Dirty Thirties.*

Farmers weren't the only people without money. Businesses and factories in the cities closed because of the Great Depression, a worldwide economic slump during the 1930s. Thousands of Albertans lost their jobs.

Alberta's economy improved during World War II (1939–1945). The drought had ended, and farmers sold grain and beef to war-torn Europe. Although no battles were fought in Canada, two large prisoner-of-war camps were built in Alberta—one in Lethbridge and one in Medicine Hat—to hold German soldiers captured overseas. Flight schools also were constructed in Alberta to train thousands of Canadian and British air-force pilots.

Two years after the war ended, Albertans discovered a large oil field in Leduc, near Edmonton. More oil, as well as natural gas, was soon found in other parts of the province. By 1956 Alberta was pumping almost 144 million barrels of oil annually.

Production increased as oil replaced coal for fueling trains and heating homes and businesses. Workers built pipelines from Edmonton to carry the valuable oil to other Canadian provinces and to the United States. By 1965 almost 1,000 oil-related companies had set up headquarters in Calgary. Edmonton became a major center for refining crude (raw) oil to be used in gasoline and other oil products.

As a result of the booming oil industry, Alberta's population grew rapidly. Immigrants from Italy, Greece, India, Sri Lanka, Great Britain, and the United States headed for Alberta. Many hoped to find jobs with oil companies.

In the mid-1960s, for the first time in the province's history, more Albertans were living in cities than in

*In 1947 hundreds of reporters, businessmen, and officials rushed to Leduc to see oil gushing from a well in a field near the town.*

small towns and on farms. By 1971 Calgary and Edmonton were among the fastest growing cities in North America. Between 1971 and 1981, Alberta's population increased from 1.6 million people to 2.2 million.

Although oil has earned a lot of money for Alberta, prices for the fuel go up and down, and supplies are limited. For this reason, Albertans have been working to develop other industries in their province. When Calgary hosted the 1988 Winter Olympic Games, for example, the province earned billions of dollars from visitors that year. Albertans hope that by developing tourism and other new industries, they will have plenty of jobs for future generations.

*Skiing is one of many activities that draw tourists to Alberta.*

*Workers in Alberta's coal mines* (below) *produce millions of tons of coal each year. Throughout the province, oil wells* (inset) *dot the landscape. Many Albertans work in cities such as Calgary* (facing page).

# *Alberta at Work*

In the 1700s, Alberta's biggest business was fur trading. By the early 1900s, most people in the province worked on ranches and farms. Nowadays, Albertans earn money from a variety of industries.

Alberta provides about 80 percent of Canada's oil and natural gas. These fuels bring in a lot of money, making Alberta one of the richest provinces in Canada. Oil is found throughout Alberta, but most oil companies are headquartered in Calgary. Thousands of miles of pipeline carry the minerals to other Canadian provinces as well as to the United States.

43

*Alberta's farmers produce many agricultural goods, including sunflowers* (above) *and beef cattle* (right).

About 69,000 people, or 5 percent of Alberta's workforce, have mining jobs. Besides exploring and drilling for oil and natural gas, miners in Alberta unearth coal, sand and gravel, and sulfur.

Digging for coal, drilling oil wells, and laying underground pipelines all disturb the land and wildlife. For this reason, mining companies in Alberta are required to restore the land to its

original state once their work is done. Topsoil is put back, seeds are planted, and any spills of oil or other polluting substances are cleaned up.

Some of Alberta's pipelines are buried under the province's rich farmland. Altogether Alberta has about 57,000 farms and ranches. They cover more than 30 percent of the province's land. Farming brings in billions of dollars for Alberta, and about 8 percent of working Albertans have jobs in agriculture.

Ranchers raise millions of beef cattle, which provide one-third of all the money made in Alberta from farming. In fact, Alberta has more beef cattle than any other province in Canada. Dairy cattle produce millions of dollars worth of milk and cream.

Wheat is Alberta's main crop. Durum wheat from Alberta is used to make pasta and bread. Farmers also grow barley and oats to feed livestock and to make cereals. Rye, another crop, is an ingredient in animal feed and in whiskey. The grain is also ground up for bread flour. Vegetables, sugar beets, canola, and sunflowers are other major crops.

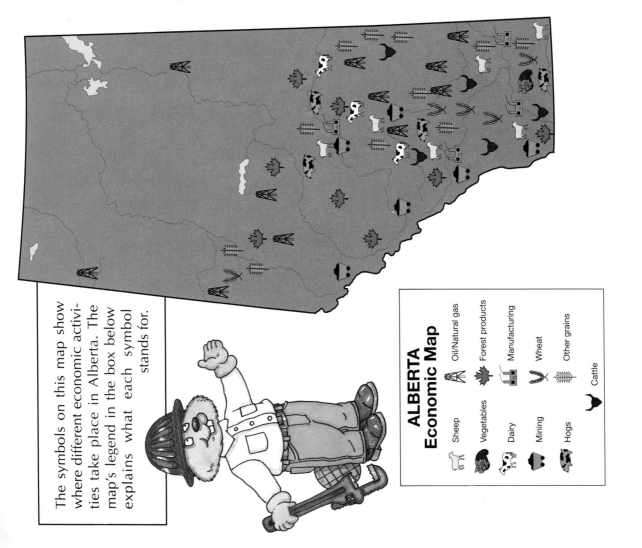

The symbols on this map show where different economic activities take place in Alberta. The map's legend in the box below explains what each symbol stands for.

**ALBERTA Economic Map**

Oil/Natural gas

Forest products

Manufacturing

Wheat

Other grains

Cattle

Sheep

Vegetables

Dairy

Mining

Hogs

*A truck hauls aspen logs to a pulp mill.*

Over the years, farming has changed Alberta's landscape. Because the plains are dry, having a dependable source of water is vital to farmers. So starting in the late 1800s, farmers in the region began to irrigate, or water, their land by building ditches and culverts (wide drainpipes) to channel water from nearby rivers to crops.

But using river water for irrigation can leave a water shortage for other uses. For this reason, many Albertans are working to conserve water so everyone will have a dependable supply.

For many years, Alberta has relied on agriculture and mining for most of its money. This is changing as the province develops new industries, such as logging. Nearly half of Alberta is forested. Although fewer than 1 percent of Alberta's workers have jobs in forestry, logging is growing quickly. Loggers in northern Alberta and in the foothills of the Rockies cut spruce, pine, fir, and aspen. Most of the timber is sawed into boards for construction or is ground into pulp for making paper.

Some Albertans worry about what will happen if too many trees are cut down. To make sure the forests will continue to grow in the future, the province requires logging companies to plant seedlings to replace felled trees.

*Some workers in Alberta manufacture chemicals.*

Many of Alberta's factories make products from the province's timber, farm goods, and oil. About 7 percent of Alberta's workforce have jobs in manufacturing. Most of these people make ethylene, methanol, and other chemicals from the province's oil.

Some factory workers in Alberta process food. They package meat, grind flour, mix feed for animals, and make cheese and other dairy products. Albertans also manufacture machinery, plastics, clothing, and wood products such as paper and lumber.

Almost three-fourths of working Albertans have service jobs helping other people or businesses. Service workers may be teachers, bankers, government officials, doctors, nurses, salespeople, bus drivers, or waiters.

# Don't Throw It Out!

In 1993 the environment club at W. D. Cuts School in St. Albert, Alberta, had a prize-winning idea for a project on waste. The club decided to look at what was being thrown away in the lunchroom at their school. Were kids wasting food? Could they reduce the amount of garbage?

Club members put on rubber gloves, removed the garbage from the bins, and separated it into categories— lunch bags, uneaten food, juice boxes, cans, glass bottles, paper, and packaging. The students found enough uneaten food to provide each student in a class of 30 with one sandwich, one juice box, and one piece of fruit!

The club then wrote a pamphlet and created posters describing their project. The pamphlet asked for ideas to reduce lunch waste and included a quiz for kids to see how much waste was in their lunches.

To reduce the number of lunch bags in the garbage, the club bought reusable nylon lunch bags and sold them to teachers, parents, and other students. For an extra fee, artists decorated the bags. In two weeks, the bags were sold out! By the end of the year, all the students at W. D. Cuts School were involved in reducing lunchroom waste. The entire school was proud when the club's project won a prize from Alberta's provincial government.

*Cooks at the Calgary Stampede rodeo are among Alberta's many service workers.*

Tourism also provides jobs for service workers in Alberta. The number of visitors traveling to Alberta has been growing since 1865. That year Alberta's first tourists—Viscount Milton and Dr. W. B. Cheadle of England—journeyed along the North Saskatchewan River to Fort Edmonton. By the 1990s, nearly 4.5 million tourists were visiting Alberta each year.

Vacationers head to Alberta to canoe or raft on the province's rivers. They hike or ride horses in the Rockies and photograph the landscape and wild animals. Skiing in Banff National Park is another popular way to enjoy the province's beauty. Visitors to Drumheller can follow the Dinosaur Trail to see remains of dinosaurs that once roamed southern Alberta. Albertans hope that in the future, tourists will continue to pay visits to this province, which is known for its scenic land and abundant resources.

*Waterton Lakes National Park* (above) *draws tourists to Alberta every year. Another popular site is the Royal Tyrrell Museum in Drumheller, where visitors can see dinosaur skeletons* (inset).

*A musician at Lake Louise* (left), *young people at Calaway Park in Calgary* (top), *a researcher in Edmonton* (below).

# The Many Faces of Alberta

At the beginning of the 1800s, Alberta's population was mostly Aboriginal. Nowadays the province's population of 2.5 million includes a variety of races and ethnic groups from all over the world. About 45 percent of the province's population have British ancestors. Other ethnic groups include people of Scottish, German, Irish, French, and Ukrainian heritage.

*Black people make up around 1 percent of Alberta's population.*

53

*Ukrainian dancers wait for their turn to perform at the Ukrainian Festival in Vegreville.*

The Ukrainian Cultural Heritage Village near Edmonton attracts thousands of visitors each year. Restored farm buildings, homes, stores, and onion-domed churches show what life in a Ukrainian village in Alberta was like during the 1800s. In nearby Vegreville, visitors can see the world's largest Ukrainian Easter egg and enjoy the Ukrainian Festival held each July.

Nowadays Aboriginal peoples make up about 3 percent of Alberta's population. They belong to many nations, including the Chipewyan, Sarcee, Beaver, Cree, Blood, Peigan, and Blackfoot. Like other Albertans, they are proud of their heritage. Many Aboriginal people are successful ranchers and ranch hands, winning prizes in Alberta's many rodeos, including the world-

*Dancing* (above) *is part of the powwow held at Head-Smashed-In Buffalo Jump. Thousands of people enjoy rodeo events* (above right) *at the Calgary Stampede.*

famous Calgary Stampede held each year in July.

Many Aboriginals meet yearly to take part in a religious ceremony called the Sun Dance. At celebrations known as powwows, visitors can watch dancing, drumming, and singing. Calgary's Glenbow Museum displays decorated tepees, costumes, tools, weapons, and other historic objects from various Aboriginal groups.

*A colorful dragon parades through Calgary's Chinatown neighborhood.*

About 40,000 Métis make their homes in Alberta. Their culture is a mix of European and Aboriginal traditions. Jigging, for example, may combine the Cree chicken dance with Scottish and French reels.

Asian residents in Alberta include Chinese, Vietnamese, Cambodians, and Laotians. Both Calgary and Edmonton have a downtown neighborhood known as Chinatown. A richly decorated red archway is one of the main attractions in Edmonton's Chinatown. Visitors in Calgary admire the Chinese Cultural Centre—a handcrafted Chinese temple.

Each August Albertans celebrate Heritage Day, a provincial holiday that

*Buffalo Lake Métis Settlement holds a rodeo every year.*

honors Alberta's rich mixture of cultures. In Edmonton, for example, thousands of people visit booths filled with ethnic crafts and food and enjoy watching dance troupes perform in colorful traditional costumes.

Alberta's communities support a variety of sports. Two National Hockey League teams—the Edmonton Oilers and the Calgary Flames—draw huge audiences of loyal fans to every game. The Calgary Stampeders and the Edmonton Eskimos battle for top honors in Canadian Football League games.

Many professionals and artists have graduated from Alberta's universities and colleges. The campuses at Grande Prairie and Lethbridge are known for fine architecture. Three agricultural colleges and the University of Alberta support research to develop new crops and animals that can survive in the province's cold weather.

Each of Alberta's ethnic groups adds its unique features to the makeup of the province. By coming together at schools, sports events, and festivals, residents share their pride in being Albertans.

*Calgary Stampeders*

*Calgary Flames*

*Calgary and Edmonton offer entertainment for adults and young people alike at jazz festivals* (above) *and children's festivals* (left).

59

# Famous Albertans

**1 Jann Arden** (born 1962) is a singer and songwriter from Calgary. Her albums include *Living under June* and *Time for Mercy,* for which she won a Juno Award in 1993.

**Barry Blanchard** (born 1960) is a mountain climber and expedition leader whose specialty is scaling dangerous peaks using very little equipment. In 1993 he set up equipment for the filming of stunts in Italy's Dolomite Mountains for the movie *Cliffhanger.* Blanchard is from Calgary.

**3 Kurt Browning** (born 1966), from Caroline, Alberta, won the Men's World Figure Skating Championship in 1989, 1990, and 1991. He has also skated in three different Winter Olympics.

**Douglas Cardinal** (born 1934) is an architect known for creating unusual curved brick buildings, such as Saint Mary's Church in his hometown of Red Deer, Alberta. In 1989 he designed the Canadian Museum of Civilization in Hull, Québec.

**5 Wilfred Carter** (born 1904) is considered one of the fathers of Canadian country-western music. Born in Nova Scotia, he began his career in Calgary in the 1920s. Some of his hits include "My Swiss Moonlight Lullaby" and "The Capture of Albert Johnson." Carter was elected to the Juno Hall of Fame in 1985.

**6** **Joe Clark** (born 1939) is a politician, author, and businessperson from High River, Alberta. He was elected six times to Canada's House of Commons between 1972 and 1993, and served briefly as the nation's prime minister from 1979 to 1980. Clark was the youngest and the first Canadian westerner to hold the office.

**7** **Crowfoot** (1830?–1890) became one of the three head chiefs of the Blackfoot nation in 1870. Born near Belly River, Alberta, he worked to maintain friendly relations with fur traders, Indian nations, and the Canadian government. In 1877 Crowfoot was a signer of Treaty No. 7, which established a Blackfoot reserve in southern Alberta.

■ **Linda Farkas** (born 1959) is an opera singer from Lethbridge, Alberta. She began her professional career in 1990, and in 1993 had a small role as a Swedish opera star in the movie *The Age of Innocence*.

■ **Don Getty** (born 1933), originally from Québec, was a quarterback with the Edmonton Eskimos football team. Named Outstanding Canadian in the Western Canadian Football League in 1959, Getty went on to become a successful businessperson and served as Alberta's premier from 1986 to 1992.

**10** **James Gladstone** (1887–1971), a member of the Blood nation, was born at Mountain Hill, North-West Territories. He was president of the Indian Association of Alberta and in 1958 became the first Aboriginal to serve in the Canadian Senate. In 1962 he helped win Canadian Indians the right to vote in national elections.

**11** **k. d. lang** (born 1961) is a singer and songwriter from Consort, Alberta. She has received many awards, including Junos in 1987 and 1990 for best country female vocalist. Her albums include *Shadowland, Absolute Torch and Twang,* and *Ingénue*.

**12** **Rhona MacKay** (born 1957, *right*) and **Robyn MacKay** (born 1959), from Cochrane, Alberta, bought the family ice-cream parlor from their mother in 1986. Each week MacKay's Cochrane Ice Cream attracts thousands of customers to the small town, located outside Calgary. In 1994 the sisters were each named Canadian Woman Entrepreneur of the Year by the University of Toronto in Ontario.

**13** **Joni Mitchell** (born 1943) is a singer and songwriter from Fort Macleod, Alberta. Among her many popular albums are *Blue, Court and Spark,* and *Clouds,* for which she won a Grammy Award in 1969.

**14** **Emily Murphy** (1868–1933), a well-known writer and legal reformer, moved to Alberta from Ontario in 1907. In 1911 she worked for the passage of the Dower Act, which protects a wife's right to a share in her husband's property. Along with four other Albertans—Henrietta Edwards, Louise McKinney, Nellie McClung, and Irene Parlby—Murphy helped win Canadian women legal recognition as "persons" in 1929.

**■** **Malcolm Norris** (1900–1967) was a brilliant speaker and politician who fought for racial equality. Born in St. Albert, Alberta, Norris was a leader in several groups, including the Indian Association of Alberta and the Métis Association of Saskatchewan.

**16** **John Dickerson ("Jackie") Parker** (born 1932) moved to Alberta in 1954 to play football with the Edmonton Eskimos. During his career, he won the Jeff Nicklin Memorial Trophy seven times and was Schenley outstanding player three times. In 1987 Parker was elected to Canada's Sports Hall of Fame.

**17 Red Crow** (1830?–1900), born at Belly River, Alberta, became chief of the Blood nation in 1870. In 1877 he signed Treaty No. 7, which set up Canada's largest reserve, located in Alberta. Red Crow helped his people maintain traditional customs and religion while adjusting to life on a reserve.

■ **Kelly Streit** (born 1968) opened a modeling agency in his hometown of Red Deer, Alberta, when he was only 18 years old. Since then, he has launched 27 Albertans—including supermodel Tricia Helfer—into successful modeling careers in New York and Paris.

**19 Gerald Tailfeathers** (1925–1975) was a professional painter and sculptor. His works show Blood people of the 1800s in battle, on the hunt, and participating in traditional ceremonies. Tailfeathers was born in Stand Off, Alberta.

**20 Guy Weadick** (1885–1953) organized the first Calgary Stampede in 1912. A cowboy born in the U.S. state of New York, Weadick owned a ranch near High River, Alberta.

■ **Anne Wheeler** (born 1946) is a filmmaker, director, producer, and writer from Edmonton. She began her career as an actress and went on to make documentaries for the National Film Board of Canada in the 1970s. Her feature films include *Loyalties* and *Cowboys Don't Cry*.

**22 Rudy Wiebe** (born 1934) writes about Canada's far north. A resident of Edmonton, he won the highly prized Governor General's Award in 1973 for his novel *The Temptations of Big Bear* and again in 1994 for *A Discovery of Strangers*.

# Fast Facts

## Provincial Symbols

**Motto:** *Fortis et Liber* (Strong and Free)
**Nickname:** Princess Province
**Flower:** wild rose
**Tree:** lodgepole pine
**Bird:** great horned owl
**Tartan:** green for the forests, gold for fields of wheat, blue for the skies and lakes, pink for the wild rose, and black for coal, petroleum, and mineral resources.

## Provincial Highlights

**Landmarks:** Badlands in the Red Deer River Valley, Icefields Parkway in Banff and Jasper National Parks, Elk Island National Park near Edmonton, Glenbow Museum in Calgary, Edmonton Space & Science Centre, West Edmonton Mall in Edmonton, Rocky Mountain House National Historic Park near Red Deer, Ukrainian Cultural Heritage Village near Edmonton

**Annual events:** Calgary Winter Festival (Feb.), Banff Festival of the Arts in Banff (June-Aug.), Klondike Days in Edmonton (July), Edmonton Folk Music Festival and the Fringe Theatre Event (Aug.), International Air Show in Red Deer (Aug.), First Night Festival in Edmonton (Dec.)

**Professional sports teams:** Edmonton Oilers, Calgary Flames (hockey); Edmonton Eskimos, Calgary Stampeders (football); Calgary Cannons, Edmonton Trappers (baseball)

## Population

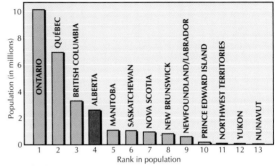

**Population\*:** 2,546,000
**Rank in population, nationwide:** 4th
**Population distribution:** 80 percent urban; 20 percent rural
**Population density:** 10.3 people per sq mi (4 per sq km)
**Capital:** Edmonton (618,195)
**Major cities (and populations\*):** Calgary (717,133), Lethbridge (63,390), Red Deer (58,656), Medicine Hat (43,807), St. Albert (42,852), Fort McMurray (34,706), Grande Prairie (28,271)
**Major ethnic groups\*:** multiple backgrounds, 42 percent; British, 20 percent; German, 7 percent; Ukrainian, 4 percent; French and Aboriginal peoples, 3 percent each; Dutch and Scandinavian, 2 percent each; Polish and Italian, 1 percent each; other single origins, 15 percent
**\*1991 census**

## Endangered Species

**Birds:** anatum peregrine falcon, mountain plover, piping plover, sage thrasher
**Plants:** slender mouse-ear-cress

## Geographic Highlights

**Area (land/water):** 255,285 sq mi (661,188 sq km)
**Rank in area, nationwide:** 6th
**Highest point:** Mount Columbia (12,293 ft/3,747 m)
**Major lakes:** Claire, Lesser Slave, Athabasca, Bistcho
**Major rivers:** North Saskatchewan, South Saskatchewan, Slave, Smoky, Hay, Peace, Athabasca, Milk

## Economy

### Percentage of Workers Per Job Sector

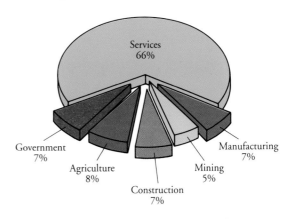

Services 66%

Government 7%

Agriculture 8%

Construction 7%

Mining 5%

Manufacturing 7%

**Natural resources:** fertile soil, oil, natural gas, coal, sand and gravel, limestone, clay, shale, salt, potash, quartz, sodium sulfate, sulfur
**Agricultural products:** beef and dairy cattle, hogs, sheep, wheat, canola, barley
**Manufactured goods:** petrochemicals and fertilizers, meats, flour, and animal feed, milk, refined petroleum, fabricated metal products, printed materials, machine tools, metal containers, structural metal

## Energy

**Electric power:** coal (88 percent), natural gas (8 percent), hydro (4 percent)

**65**

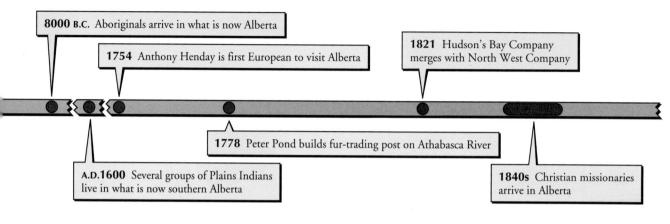

**8000 B.C.** Aboriginals arrive in what is now Alberta

**1754** Anthony Henday is first European to visit Alberta

**1821** Hudson's Bay Company merges with North West Company

**1778** Peter Pond builds fur-trading post on Athabasca River

**A.D.1600** Several groups of Plains Indians live in what is now southern Alberta

**1840s** Christian missionaries arrive in Alberta

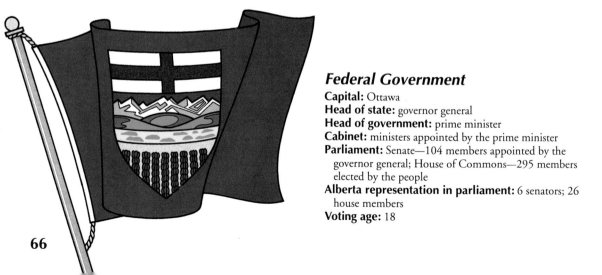

### *Federal Government*

**Capital:** Ottawa
**Head of state:** governor general
**Head of government:** prime minister
**Cabinet:** ministers appointed by the prime minister
**Parliament:** Senate—104 members appointed by the governor general; House of Commons—295 members elected by the people
**Alberta representation in parliament:** 6 senators; 26 house members
**Voting age:** 18

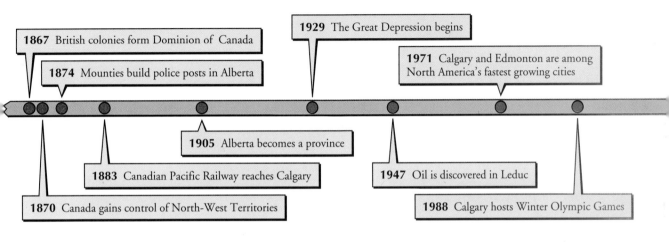

**1867** British colonies form Dominion of Canada

**1874** Mounties build police posts in Alberta

**1929** The Great Depression begins

**1971** Calgary and Edmonton are among North America's fastest growing cities

**1905** Alberta becomes a province

**1883** Canadian Pacific Railway reaches Calgary

**1870** Canada gains control of North-West Territories

**1947** Oil is discovered in Leduc

**1988** Calgary hosts Winter Olympic Games

## *Provincial Government*

**Capital:** Edmonton
**Head of state:** lieutenant governor
**Head of government:** premier
**Cabinet:** ministers appointed by the premier
**Legislative Assembly:** 83 members elected to terms that can last up to five years
**Voting age:** 18
**Major political parties:** Progressive Conservative, Liberal, Reform

## *Government Services*

To help pay the people who work for Alberta's government, Albertans pay taxes on money they earn and on many of the items they buy. The services run by the provincial government help assure Albertans of a high quality of life. Government funds help pay for medical care, for education, for road building and repairs, and for other facilities such as libraries and parks. In addition, the government has funds to help people who are disabled, elderly, or poor.

# *Glossary*

**chinook**  A warm dry wind that blows down the eastern slopes of the Rocky Mountains, usually in winter and early spring.

**colony**  A territory ruled by a country some distance away.

**drought**  A long period of extreme dryness due to lack of rain or snow.

**glacier**  A large body of ice and snow that flows down mountain valleys, often following paths originally formed by rivers. The term is also used to refer to masses of ice that move slowly over the land's surface.

**ice age**  A period when ice caps cover large regions of the earth's surface. The term *Ice Age* usually refers to the most recent one, called the Pleistocene, which began almost 2 million years ago and ended about 10,000 years ago.

**ice cap**  A very thick, slow-moving glacier that covers large areas of a continent.

**immigrant**  A person who moves into a foreign country and settles there.

**missionary**  A person sent out by a religious group to spread its beliefs to other people.

**prairie**  A large area of level or gently rolling grassy land with few trees.

**precipitation**  Rain, snow, and other forms of moisture that fall to earth.

**reserve**  Public land set aside by the government to be used by Aboriginal peoples.

**treaty**  An agreement between two or more groups, usually having to do with peace or trade.

# *Pronunciation Guide*

**Aboriginal**  (a-buh-RIH-juh-nuhl)

**Assiniboine**  (uh-SIH-nuh-boyn)

**Athabasca**  (a-thuh-BAS-kuh)

**Chipewyan**  (chih-puh-WY-uhn)

**Gros Ventre**  (GROH-vahnt)

**Kootenay**  (KOOT-ihn-ay)

**Laotian**  (lay-OH-shuhn)

**Leduc**  (luh-DOOK)

**Peigan**  (pee-GAN)

**Sarcee**  (SAHR-see)

**Vegreville**  (VEHG-uhr-vihl)

# Index

# About the Author

Sarah Yates has been a writer and editor for more than 20 years. She has published articles for a variety of magazines, newspapers, and journals. Among her books are two children's titles, *Can't You Be Still?* and *Nobody Knows!* A resident of Winnipeg, Manitoba, Ms. Yates practices puppetry and enjoys playing with her daughter and other children.

# Acknowledgments

Laura Westlund, pp. 1, 3, 64–67; Steve Warble/Mountain Magic, pp. 2, 8; Jerry Hennen, pp. 6, 14 (inset, top), 16–17, 42 (inset, top), 44, 51, 71; Terry Boles, pp. 7, 10, 46, 65 (bottom left); David Dvorak, Jr., pp. 12, 13, 14 (center and inset, bottom), 15, 69; Mapping Specialists Ltd., pp. 10, 11, 46; George Wuerthner, p. 16 (inset); Alberta Tourism, p. 17 (inset); Charles Truscott, p. 18; © Eliot Cohen, p. 19; Provincial Museum of Alberta, Edmonton, Alberta, p. 21; Whyte Museum of the Canadian Rockies, Banff, Alberta, S. J. Thompson, p. 23; Hudson's Bay Company Archives, Provincial Archives of Manitoba, pp. 24, 25; National Archives of Canada: p. 26 (C15244), p. 27 (C82974), p. 35 (C56088); Provincial Archives of Alberta, Photo Collection: p. 28 (OB2562), p. 38 (A4509), p. 40 (P2721), p. 61 (center right, J4579/11), p. 63 (top left, B1054), p. 63 (center, A8589); Glenbow Archives, Calgary, Alberta: p. 29 (NA–550–18), pp. 30–31 (NA–140–1), p. 39 (NA–1831–1), p. 60 (bottom, NA–2771–1), p. 61 (top, NA–29–1), p. 61 (center left, NA–4212–154), p. 63 (top right, NA–1483–10); Provincial Archives of Manitoba: p. 32, Transportation, 2/23 (N16477), photo by A. B. Thom, p. 33 (bottom), Simons, Marguerite, C26/7, p. 33 (inset), High River 2, (N1392), photo by Steele and Co.; McCord Museum of Canadian History, Notman Photographic Archives, p. 34; Marie Mills/David Cummings, p. 37; Mike Ridewood, Calgary Convention & Visitors Bureau, pp. 41, 43, 52 (top right), 53, 55 (left), 56, 59 (both); Robert E. Cramer/Geographical Slides, p. 42 (bottom); Industry, Science and Technology Canada, pp. 44–45, 48, 52 (bottom), 54; Alberta Pacific Forest Industries Inc., p. 47; Katie Boyd/W. D. Cuts School, St. Albert, AB, p. 49; Calgary Stampede, pp. 50, 55 (right); © James P. Rowan, p. 51 (inset); © Judith Jango-Cohen, p. 52 (left); Community Services/Buffalo Lake Métis Settlement, p. 57; Calgary Convention & Visitors Bureau, p. 58 (both); Andrew MacNaughton, p. 60 (top); F. Scott Grant/Canadian Sport Images, p. 60 (center); Hollywood Book & Poster, pp. 61 (bottom), 62 (center left); Winter Photographics, p. 62 (top); BC Archives & Records Service, p. 62 (center right, 39854); Edmonton Eskimos, p. 62 (bottom); Larry Towell, p. 63 (bottom); Gerry Kopelow/Photographics, Inc., p. 72.